Molly Case is a spoken word artis
b

Sl
Li
tv
U
ar

In
he
ga
Fc
th

Sl
Ti
th
Bl
hc
th

In
hc
be
to

THIS BOOK IS PART OF
ISLINGTON READS BOOKSWAP
SCHEME

Please take this book and either return it to a
Bookswap site or replace with one of your own
books that you would like to share.

If you enjoy this book, why not join your local
Islington Library and borrow more like it for free?

Find out about our FREE e-book,
e-audio, newspaper and
magazine apps, activities for
pre-school children and other
services we have to offer at
www.islington.gov.uk/libraries

ISLINGTON
For a more equal future

Underneath the Roses Where I Remembered Everything

Molly Case

Burning Eye

This edition published by Burning Eye Books 2015
www.burningeye.co.uk

@burningeyebooks

Burning Eye Books
15 West Hill, Portishead, BS20 6LG

ISBN 978 1 90913 6 632

Life is only comprehensible through a thousand local gods...
spirits of certain trees, of certain curves of brick wall, of certain
fish-and-chip shops, if you like and slate roofs, frowns in people,
slouches. I'd say to them: "Worship all you can see and more
will appear."

Peter Shaffer, Equus.

CONTENTS

*To my wonderful family
who supported me every step of the way
through the nursing journey
and to the incredible 5/12 cohort
who no doubt have their own stories to tell...*

THE PARK NEXT TO THE HOSPITAL

The park holds our memories
like beads of rain
on scaffolding,
each one hanging there
grappling
for space.

Stars hole-punched
the sky
above the common;
we watched
traces of meteors
and Boeing 747s
headed to Heathrow.
The moon is
a cut-out chip of bone
alone against the night
as we were,
breath
suspended,
chip-shop chips
ketchup and Coke cans
upended.
Where we smoked
and drank
whiskey from flasks,
basked in the glow
of cigarettes sparked
here, after dark.
Where braille-like bark
lost the curlings and
intricacies that made
daytime landmarks,
now
unrecognisable,
so we linked arms,
felt safe,
felt stable.

The itch
of school-shirt
shop labels,
eight pm in raggedy
school clothes,
trainers
with fat laces
tied and twisted
like Croydon's
tram cables.

I have been here
before,
in lives
that whirred past
like revolving doors.
The park next to the hospital:
the one place for sure
to stay the same,
it's crusted with fossil fuels
and mineral jewels
set alight,
burning
like an eternal flame –
reminding us
of the one place
we know
will always
stay the same.

This is where
we learnt to kiss;
there was Gemma
and Scott,
and I kissed Chris.
Washing-machine tongues
told by Hannah to
do it like this.

Baggies of weed
that was
once just oregano;
we smoked
it up anyway,
leapt the riverbanks
like archipelagos,
pretending to
be lean though
we knew we weren't,
but none of it mattered
because this is where
we learnt
about life,
in lunch breaks
and after school
shrugged off
homework,
school dinners
and rules.
Where we witnessed that
one fight we thought
would end it all –
that rapid punch
that left Lee sprawled
on the grass,
clutching his skull.
We dispersed
like squawking gulls
who actually
never left;
the common was their
canteen and
their hobby was theft.
Brown bread crusts,
Wagon Wheel husks,
chip sticks,
carrot sticks,

Turkey Twizzlers slick
with grease,
chicken wings,
50p a piece,
running from
police
who weren't
even chasing us
but it made us
look cool to the kids
on the bus.

Enough, I think,
stop… right… there,
these memories
could leave me
gasping for air,
and I know that when
I look back
the park will still be there:
The Park Next to the Hospital
that I now work in.
I'm ready for the next bit,
for more memories to begin.

WELCOME TO PARADISE

4th of November, 2012

06.10 Wake up twenty minutes before the alarm, nervous about new placement in a nursing home.

06.15 Have tea and cereal. The milk looks grey in the curtainy gloom.

06.30 Slip into scratchy uniform and tight trousers, fix all bits: fob watch, badge, lanyard, pens, torch.

06.45 Brush teeth, put make-up on, leave. Still nervous.

07.30 Park up the road and make my way to the nursing home. It's raining, the dockyard chimneys shine like wet clay against the sky. A boarded-up house has *Welcome to Paradise graffitied on the door.*

07.35 Sign in at the desk and ask for the manager. She won't be here until nine. Sit and read *The Shining.*
Tough old world, baby. If you're not bolted together tightly, you're gonna shake, rattle, and roll before you turn thirty.
I'm always early. I stare at the stuffed scarecrow sitting opposite me. A sign reading *Well Meadows Care Home* hangs around its neck. It has stitched buttons for eyes.

07.50 Make my way to the first floor.

07.53 Find another human being wandering the corridors. Introduce myself. She says, 'Go and sit somewhere. The manager won't be here until nine.'

08.00 Go and sit somewhere. Continue reading *The Shining.* *Sometimes human places, create inhuman monsters.*

08.14 Handover. Two nurses arrive in the room; neither looks at me. Turn the page.

08.30   Handover is finished. Nurse A says, 'You might as well come with me now.' I try to read her name badge.

08.40   Am piled up with towels, pads, and clean clothes and sent into room 4: lovely room with all the service user's belongings inside. Feel like I shouldn't be here like this.

08.42   Nurse A says, 'You will help me wash this man. What's your name again?'
        'Molly.'

08.43   Assist Nurse A with washing and dressing the service user. Chat to him about wartime in Germany and about Lancashire, where they make the towels he uses. They're the softest in England. Start feeling a bit better.

09.15   Two carers are in the lounge, more service users arrive for breakfast. I stand there seeing what needs to be done.

09.17   Grab a blue apron and start pouring tea.
        'He doesn't have tea, he has coffee,' says a carer.
        Put teapot down and stand and watch.
        Serve porridge.
        Help a lady eat her breakfast.

09.30   *Sit with service users, watch Jeremy Kyle and This Morning.*

10.30   Read the *Daily Mail*, nasty headlines.

11.05   Talk to a service user about her dog back home but speak quietly as everybody is asleep.

11.10   Read the noticeboard, walk up the corridor, wonder when the manager will get here. Wish somebody would talk to me. Look for the toilets.

11.30   Manager arrives, all in red.
         'I'm Jane.'
         'Hello, I'm Molly.'
         'You've settled in well.'
         'I'm okay. I'm just helping some of the service users.'
         'Good. It's good to get involved. You must get
         involved.'
         'Okay.'

11.35   The service users are asleep. Ask the carer if we
         should do any activities. 'Not until three o'clock.'
         Watch a John Wayne film. The technicolour looks
         beautiful. Brown mountains, a river raging white.

12.40   I contact another student on my phone. Can't wait to
         hear from her. She has the same placement.
         *Are you here at Well Meadow Nursing Home? Please
         tell me how you're finding it – feels like nobody
         knows I'm even here yet! Scared! xx*

12.43   Knock on the office door. Nurse A looks up.
         'Hi, I just wondered whether you are my mentor?'
         'No, no more students. I already have two. I don't
         know about any more.'
         'Should I ask the manager?'
         No answer. Looks back to the screen.

12.45   Decide to find manager and ask about mentorship
         and my shifts.

12.48   Knock knock.
         'Did you want to see me?'
         'Not really.'
         'Maybe about who I'm working with or my rota?'
         'It's Nurse A upstairs; she is your mentor.'
         'Oh, I don't think she's aware of that...'
         'She is. We will work out your rota later.'
         'Would you mind coming upstairs with me and just
         checking she's okay with it?'

12.55   Stand in the office upstairs. Nurse A and manager sit
         at desk.
         'She is your new student.'
         Points at me.
         'No, I already have two. No more.'
         Puts her head in her hands.
         'I don't want more students. I don't like students.'
         'She is yours.'
         'Excuse me,' I say. 'I'm sorry but I don't think this
         lady wants to mentor me. I don't feel comfortable in
         here…'
         'She will mentor you.'
         'Okay.'
         Manager leaves.
         Nurse A starts typing.

13.00   Read the noticeboard again.

13.07   Lunchtime. Help a service user to eat and we chat
         about why we eat fish and chips on Fridays.

14.30   Nurse A, my mentor, brings the drug trolley out.
         'Should I shadow you whilst you do medication?'
         'No.'

15.00   Service users go downstairs for activities.
         Ask carer whether I should attend too.
         'You better stay up here with your mentor, just in
         case…'

15.05   Ask Nurse A whether she would like me to help her
         with anything in the office.
         'It depends on what you want to learn.'
         'What are you doing at the moment?'
         'Care plan.'
         'Can I have a look at some?'
         No answer.
         I sit and read some care plans.

16.00   Nurses' meeting downstairs: they talk about a service user drinking too much Coke and two service users arguing whether *Emmerdale* should have the subtitles on or not. The room is hot with breath. Wish I could open the window. They mention a service user with swollen legs who says she wants to die. They discuss footstools. Want to ask them to talk more about her fears and anxieties.

16.15   Another nurse mentions one of the service users has a grade two pressure sore.
'But it was grade one on Monday,' Nurse B says.
The room looks shocked.
A first-year student reported this pressure area on Monday.
Feel very sorry for the service user with the pressure sore.

16.58   Receive a message on my phone:
It's awful! They don't want us there. What are we going to do? When I try and help Nurse B says I'm working above my ability and when I don't, she says I'm lazy! xx
Me: *I'm so happy to hear from you, just glad there's somebody else here! xx*

17.00   Teatime. I help to feed a service user. Mash potato in soup.

17.46   Look at the clock.

18.00   Pass the clinical room where Nurses B and C are.
Nurse B is shouting, 'They are useless, these students.'
I look in at them as I pass. She shouts 'USELESS' at me and pretends to spit on the floor. Keep walking.
Sit on the toilet and wonder whether that actually happened.

18.05   Wish I could go home. Think about all the people I love and who love me and feel a bit better. This is temporary. Three more weeks, just three weeks…

18.06   Take paracetamol for a headache. Leave the toilets.

18.20   A man asks to go to his room. I offer to take him and to give him a hand with anything he needs before bed. A carer comes and takes over. 'Thanks anyway,' she says.

18.24   Sit on a footstool and watch the ITV news.

19.00   Watch *Emmerdale.*

19.30   Watch *Eastenders.* It's rubbish. It's always rubbish.

19.58   Let home early. Take the opportunity. The air outside feels great; clean after rain.

20.00   Get in the car. Welcome to Paradise.

CLODAGH

Friday, 18.03,
London Bridge station;
it's the hottest summer in years.
Poker-hot,
train tracks and gears,
businessmen laughing
cracking open beers,
cheers of crowds
off to watch the football.

Spilling out onto the platform
we are a piebald snake,
heat-drunk and slow,
no idea of which direction to go.
And then I hear it:
crackled-tin
over the tannoy –
grated alloy,
voice sharp and spurred:
'Platform Three is in need of a doctor,
a doctor or a nurse.'
That's me, I guess.
There might be something I can do.
So I think of all the studying
and the exams I've sat through.

There's a woman on Platform Three
who is drunk and would rather be
left alone.
Fifties, small, hung head, nothing said
except for the police officer on his phone.

'Yeah, mate, we've had her before,
you know the score,
she's clearly Oliver Twist.'

I wander up nervously
tuning in to what I've missed.

'Yeah, just ask her a few questions, love,
all of the above,
I'm sure you know
what to say.'

So I ask her if she's got pain anywhere.
Her skin is mottled and grey.
'Are you diabetic,
are you short of breath,
has this happened before?'

'I just want to get home,' she says.
'I don't want to be here anymore.
Yeah, I've had drinks and
I'm tired of you asking...
what's my name...
is that what you said?'

I nod my head
though can see she's frustrated.
I sit back on haunches,
listening, waiting.

'My name is Clodagh
and I'm from Donnybrook.'
The officer sits down next to me,
gives me a look,
whispers in my ear a thistle
of prickly words:

'She's violent, a right headcase,'
(are the things I heard).
'Likes crack and alcohol too,
she's already known to authorities,
so not a lot else we can do?
Save, eject her from here,
lock her up for the night.
I mean, look, what a sight:

smackhead, total nutter,
sometimes they're better off
just left in the gutter.'

I look at Clodagh, at
her eyes red-rimmed and raw,
and I hear something
she's saying, not aloud,
though I can't be sure.

Don't you know who I am, officer?
Do you know where I've come from?
Sometimes we are bigger than this,
than labels and preconceptions.
I am Clodagh from Donnybrook
and my mother named me this.
I remember cockles and mussels,
her sweetened Kerry-lily kiss.

And, officer, my grandfather was one
of your types too,
but he played hopscotch
with street kids,
drank the whole night through.
Did you know my father?
He could smoke a pipe
underwater
and I am his daughter,
Clodagh,
from Donnybrook
near the bay
and my grandfather could catch
a whole raft of trout for dinner
using grenades to blast them his way.
You see, he was a police chief;
looked after the English
in the Troubles,
was there when

O'Mulligan's bar
became a smoking pile of rubble.
He kept two shotguns
above his door,
scared of assassination,
a Colt .45 in a hidden location
and a .32 above the crucifix
for luck
and salvation.

'See what I mean, love?
She's clearly pissed as a fart
and I'm not staying here
at London Bridge
waiting for trouble to start.
I don't think she's got anyone,
though I know she ain't homeless –
hostel or bedsit, couch, just a guess.
People like this have friends like
kite tails, you know, they drift away.'

Again I hear Clodagh
and the words
she seems to say.

Have you ever known what it's like
to never see someone again?
The person you loved the most,
your family, your friend?
Well, Dad said working in a lighthouse
was the only job Billy could do.
Something about the holes
in his head,
the way light
just shone through.
So he went away
(I never saw him again)
to Poolbeg lighthouse

on a pier
off Dublin bay.
Billy was the tallest,
falling over his laces,
would thread daisies
in his button holes
and weave long grass
round his braces.

Dublin Bay was beautiful at night,
shaped like a horseshoe
so you could see
every flickering light,
not just Billy's lighthouse,
but the bonfires
that lined the coast.
And sometimes
when the mist
swept off the water
I could have sworn
I saw his ghost.

Don't you know who I am, officer?
Do you know where I've come from?
Sometimes we are bigger than this,
than labels and preconceptions.
I am Clodagh from Donnybrook
and my mother named me this.
Sometimes it's worth listening
to the rest of it 'cause you don't know
what you've missed.

PECKHAMPLEX CAR PARK
For Damilola Taylor[1]

There is a spot on top of PeckhamPlex car park
where I go and stand sometimes –
a bit of a climb since the lift is broken,
but it's worth it for the unspoken
secret that is this
view of London,
of our home
where chicken shops and acetone,
cobbled streets and gas lamps
ignite our bones.
And up here where autumn
or spring is letter-boxed
between concrete earth
and concrete sky,
the sun on the Shard
broken open,
a jagged eye,
high above the noise,
I watch rainbow-necked
pigeons fly.
But it often gets me thinking
of the little boy that died,
killed in this city
fourteen years ago
in a place so far from his birth.
Sometimes I think this, up here?
This could be the end of the earth.

[1] *I didn't know Damilola Taylor, nor did I know his family or his experiences. At the time of his death he was ten and I was eleven and I remember, as a child, being struck by this detail, scared and confused by what had happened to this poor little boy in a city we both lived in.*

NURSING THE NATION

A woman comes in,
too young to bear this;
she's got a disease that will make her miss –
her daughter's wedding day,
her first grandchild being born.
How would that feel, to have that all torn
away from you?

I can't answer that question,
it's not my place to say,
but I can tell you what we did for her,
how we helped her get through the day.
A cup of tea there and one for all her family,
as they came, throughout the night,
what a sight; there were loads of them.
To help her fight the awful pain of it,
paying last visits, we wouldn't let them miss it –
farewell from a brother,
last kisses with their mother –
holiest love, love like no other.

Maybe there's bad ones,
no doubt that there are,
but for this list I'm writing
we don't want the same tar-brush,
crushing our careers before they've even started;
how could you say this
about people so big-hearted?
Who would have thought we'd be having to defend?
We don't do this for our families,
we don't do this for our friends,
but for strangers.
Because this is our vocation
and we're sick and tired
of being told we don't do enough for this nation.
So listen to us, hear us goddamn roar;
you say we're not doing enough?
Then we promise we'll do more.
This time, next time,

there's nothing we can't handle,
even if you bring us down,
show us scandal, scandal, scandal.

You remember that man covered in burns head to toe?
I don't think you do
'cause you were on that TV show:
lipgloss-kissed women on daytime TV,
come into our world, see things that we see.

One lady, passing, had no relatives to stay.
We sang her to sleep, let angels take her away.
Were you there that day when we held her hand?
Told her nothing would harm her,
that there was a higher plan.
Saw her face as she remembered a faith she'd once held,
watched her breath in the room as she finally exhaled.

Why don't you meet us? Come, shake our hands.
Try to fit it in between having tea with your fans.
Your hands are so soft and mine are cracked.
Why don't you let us on air?
Let us air the facts.

We've washed and shrouded people
that we've never known,
pinned flowers to the sheet
and told them they're still not alone.
Shown families to the faith room
and watched them mourn their dead,
then got back to work, bathed patients, made beds.

Hindus, Muslims, Jews and Sikhs,
Buddhists and Christians and just people off the street,
we've cared for them all and we love what we do,
we don't want a medal, we just want to show you.
So listen to us, hear us goddamn roar;
you say we're not doing enough?
Then we promise we'll do more.

MISSING BEATS

Cannula in the right arm,
and nil by mouth since six;
you're waiting till the afternoon
for your heart to be fixed.
See, it doesn't beat right,
the electrics trip and skip
and with a heart rate of 140
you lie back tired
on hospital sheets,
thinking of all the things
you've ever missed
with a circuit board
that lies incomplete.

And now the doctor says
you're having six-second pauses,
that's why, he says,
you're feeling so nauseous
but don't worry,
'cause we know
what the cause is.
It's that your electrics are
bucking,
they're feral
and lawless,
careering away from us
like frightened wild horses.

Three o'clock and time
for the pacemaker fitting.
I go down with you,
sitting
leant against the bed.
You tell me
that all the words the doctor said
are now blurring
in your head.

You say,
'What happens in those pauses,
those beats I've missed
and skipped?'
and I feel like I should
have an answer for this,
some words of comfort
from a nursing script.
You say, 'Time has gotten
away from me.
What if all the missed beats
add up to moments that can never be
retrieved,
that I can never
get back,
never to be rewound,
laughed at,
labelled and stacked
to watch again?
Missed beats,
missing memories
that I search for in vain...'
But it's time to go in,
the catheter lab awaits,
patient table,
X-ray scanner and screen,
volt machine
to fix your heart rate.
There's emergency drugs
laid out on the side,
leads and wires
ready to be tied
and stitched,
switched on and fixed
through voltmeter twitches
back to a normal heart rate
no longer
troubled by glitches.

And all of this will happen
whilst you're awake,
a life-saving operation
but one that is making you shake
with nerves.
They give you a little sedation,
wait, watch and observe
and when you're settled
the surgeon
makes his first incision,
a gentle curve
in the anaesthetised site
just above the heart
a little to his right.
Later, the first volt is given,
we watch on the screen
and none of us can believe
what happens.
White noise for a minute,
then the screen turns black
but after a second
an image comes back.
A little girl in blue
walking alone
along a railway line,
looks like summer,
cloudless sky and pines.

'What's going on?
I can feel something happening.'
Your voice from beneath the sheet
and none of us say anything,
the surgeon's taken a seat.

Another volt;
another image on the screen,
played out to us like
a programme on TV.

This time, point of view
looking upwards
from below,
legs in wellies,
the arch of a shelter,
and the glow
from bombers flying far too low.
You pull back the sheet now
so you can see the screen
just at the moment it all fades to green.
'My memories!' you say,
as there comes another scene
for us to watch:
the trees below, a car driving
over Hammersmith flyover,
a journey you know.
It's you and your father
visiting Granddad in his
mansion-block flat on a Sunday
but wanting to stay
at home
where Mum is cooking a roast.

'I can't believe it,' you say
but the volts keep coming,
the machine is humming,
running reels of memories
past our eyes:
you at five learning the alphabet,
the smell of the plastic letters
that sometimes even today
is carried to you on the air
(though you can't place it).
Battersea funfair,
learning to smoke,
the purple raincoat
your mother made,
the Beatles,

third kisses,
fourth and fifth in the rain,
the tiny flat above the greengrocer's
where you got locked out
again and again,
ripping open wedding presents,
unable to contain happiness.
Sitting in the garden
with pain in your chest
wondering when you get the results of the tests…

'They're all there,' you cry, 'they've come back to me,'
and by now everybody in the theatre
has stood up to see
your face:
joyful and alive,
lost memories revived,
and all the things you thought
you had lost
are intact and gleaming.
'They're back,' you say, 'they survived.'

THE BLACK HOLE

Aqualand,
south of France, 1999 –
I've just braved Niagara
and I'm feeling fine.

Jump to now and it's a different time –
nursing: the first time I see somebody die
and all I can think about
is the summer of '99
and the rush and the pull of the water slides.

I can almost hear them
through the syringe beeps
and on-call doctor bleeps:
a hundred bare feet slapping across the parc,
a splash and a shout intercepted by a laugh.
Anaconda is to the left
and King Cobra twists above our heads
but I'm looking over at the dark slide
with the mountains behind,
looks like one of a kind,
black-out paint and shining
wet like killer-whale skin.
I think about changing my mind,
turning round,
back to the technicolour gleam
and sun-warmed plastic
of Twister and the Splash 'n' Scream.

Jump to now:
I'm looking at the tiny rash
that has developed underneath the needle,
the needle that's giving enough medicine
to keep him drifting just below the surface.
He's with us, but he's not,
like words drawn in the sand
and now that the waves have come,
they're almost long forgot.

I wonder what it's like standing at the edge,
hovering between life and death,
one final breath catching on
the ribcage hinges welding
the now with what's ahead.

Hovering at the top of the slide,
the black-out one
with nuts and bolts on the outside,
I'm scared –
staring into a canyon of black nights,
deep and fast, and swallowing the light.
The Black Hole, it's called –
and I can't tell what's beyond it.

Back at the hospital bedside
there are now so few breaths
I wonder if he's living on something else instead.

Holding breath, *The Black Hole* gapes at me,
it's clear to see
it's time to pass through
and though I'm still scared
and my feet are being pulled away from me
I think maybe I'll travel so fast I'll start to feel… free?

I look back over my shoulder;
ah, I don't want to leave this behind.
If I go now,
I'll never find my way back.
There's sun loungers and fake sand,
chips with so much salt
they leave whole crystals in your hands.
The sun is warm on my skin
and I can't imagine
not feeling that again.

Somebody places a kiss on his head,
holds his hand, rests a flower
and a photograph on top of the bed.
They tell him about his life

and the things he's been through
and I can see that all you've ever needed
is now right here with you.

And then I realise everybody I have ever loved
is going to live on inside me.
Maybe not in any way I can touch or see,
but I know they're there
and, buoyant and lifted,
I feel cradled in mid-air.
I let go and The Black Hole takes me;
for a moment I feel goosebumps
as I lose the warmth of the sun
but then I think about the people
waiting at the bottom:
my sister, my dad, my mum.

I am travelling back and forth,
a wave shucking across sea-worn stones
waiting to be thrown,
a child skims me
across the surface and now –
I am a wind-blown leaf,
watching the world unravel beneath me,
where bulrushes and brambles
catch feathers in their tangles,
now trampled down into muddy mounds,
worms waiting to be found by brittle beaks,
and though I can't speak,
I know that I am the sound of the earth,
I am the dew, the grass, the first
light that flinks through curtain cracks
when morning comes.

And look, there I am:
grinning, whooshing down Niagara,
my photo stuck to the fridge,
Blu-Tacked in time:
the year of Aqualand,
summer '99.

SHIPWRECK

Your chest is buoyant,
an iron-belted barrel
that rises and expands,
my hands are laid
upon flotsam ribs
and jetsam squib –
the spark and arc of a current
traversing your heart:
I felt it – a firework.

Cut out from your horizon,
I know these countries so well –
smell minerals and soil,
your skin oils like
soaked oak decks after rain.
And again, I felt it –
this is what ancient
gods have in their veins,
the same as us:
dust motes and love notes
trapped in glass bottles
glinting in the sun.
I think I may have known your body
before my own was one.

Our sun-dried sheets
are taut beneath open thighs;
outside the sky
is sheltering the sun,
casting white-hot caps of light
on our surface.

And now,
hard as timber,
guided as steady
as the vertex of the bow,
we, ghost-ship,
sail up beyond

the lip of matter,
floating there,
suspended in mid-air –
toes curling in like a sea anemone.
Inside you glide through
to the heart of me,
green moons, wet mouths
a slick that travels south,
limbs like storm-beaten wood,
rucked up,
tangled and tired,
no good for a while…

Shipwreck, we are all that's left
and moored on a sand spit
as the waves keep coming in,
I listen to the sound of you
and all that has ever been.

NIGHT SHIFT ON THE DEMENTIA FLOOR

Tonight I work the night shift –
the graveyard shift.
Except, when you die at 3.52,
there is no grave marker above your bed.
Grey-darker, your skin fades;
there is no yard to lay you to rest, just yet.
Outside only estate houses run by the council,
white flat-board walls and paper doors –
the road beside them.

The night-wind blows hard tonight;
I hear the whistle through hollow caverns –
paper doors, paper chest.
I lift thin cotton nightdress, thermal vest,
to feel your skin rise and fall,
rise and fall –
and then nothing.
There is no movement –
nothing at all.
I feel every bone in your hand
like bird-bones, so small.
The shadow of our hands
entwined against the wall,
as if they're flying up past the brickwork,
taking your mind higher than it could ever go here.

I look down at you on the bed;
your navel staring up at me,
a hollow eye –
a tunnel connecting you
directly back to your birth,
to a time when your mind was soft.
Unprotected by unformed bones,
joins not yet filled
but looked after
by people who loved you.
People with strong wills
and intentions to keep you safe,

whilst you grew harder –
formed skeletal scaffolds around your mind.
And then came the time
those bones broke in your mind
or perhaps it became too strong;
the spirit behind the bones
began to unwind.
Too good for its cage,
too powerful for those things,
it got stronger than bone,
caught fire, grew wings.

And staring into your third hollow eye,
I watch your mind break free,
with wings against the walls,
out across the skyscape,
rise and fall –
casting great shadows and shapes,
blanketing the whole world in cumulus drapes.

THE CALL

I was spending four days
with the paramedics,
part of my academic elective
to see what their job was like,
to see the type of people they meet –
excited for 80mph blue-lighting
down the streets of London.
From chest pain
to aneurisms and broken veins,
fakers feigning faints,
gym sprains
and drunk city workers
slumped down in the rain,
I was loving it.

Until one call left me split
wide open,
couldn't rid the thought of it
from my mind,
the unexpectedness
of what we were to find,
the smell of it unwinding
down the street,
our steel-toed boots,
rubber soles running in on the concrete.

The call had been:
FEMALE 20% BURNS.
'Ahh, eight in the morning, nah – you'll learn
this will be pretty easy,' they said, 'I bet it will, you'll see.'
But when we pulled up
with the helicopter behind us,
we knew it wouldn't be…

Squat terrace house with the door open,
we could see right through
to a darkened kitchen area
now flickering in ambulance blue.

There, on a stool,
with the floor soaking wet
was somebody I knew I'd never forget.
Pale-naked from the waist up,
face up,
palms up
like empty eggshells,
with burnt skin now thick
as a rhino hide,
yellowing at the edges,
pinker where peeled skin
revealed the inside.
Burnt: her neck, chest, her arms, but
she was unmoving, current-less, calm.

Her grandchildren sat high on worktops,
swinging their legs,
reminding me of childhood games:
shark-infested waters,
or lava… or flames.
And they didn't know
what had happened to their grandma,
no landmarks,
only an expressionless face,
eyes as white and round as headlamps –
out of place –
with no light there,
just two globes that didn't blink, just stared.
Burnt hair: a black crust
that fell away with the slightest knock,
shocked-still, and that sulphuric stink,
an acrid trace
that lay thick enough to taste.

'She was smoking a fag in her bedroom, next thing we know
the fire alarm is going, we ran downstairs, saw her on fire,
covered in flames, but she wasn't screaming. I was shouting,
calling her name. Her reaction times are slow to pain, it's this

disease she's got, a disease in her brain. She won't scream, she
won't scream…'

The paramedics wrapped her skin in cling film
to ease the nerve endings,
keep the fluid in.
She was translucent,
collarbone-thin
and freezing from being doused in water.
I tried to concentrate
through the keening of her daughter.

We got her on the back of the ambulance;
she was still silent as an oak.
Later we learned her airway
had swollen shut from all the smoke.
There were no veins accessible to give her pain relief,
her daughter cried fat tears heavy with grief
and the little girl's hands were trembling,
tiny shudders like a breeze-blown leaf.

Enveloped into hospital, then
we were off somewhere new,
another scald, another cut,
a patient with lips turning blue.
It's a call I'll always remember
and I hope that she's okay,
but I know they'll never forget the fire
and the horror of that day.

SPINAL

Today I watched a spinal block,
bupivacaine anaesthetic
to take away the shock
of surgery, four hands on skin,
fine needle as quivering and thin
as a web laid across an autumn leaf.
We lay you on your side,
put sheets and slides underneath:
ready for the procedure.
I whisper in your ear,
'We're not going to leave ya,
you're safe here,
just relax, breathe slow.'
The anaesthetist tells me about ratio:
Poiseuille's equation, the way the liquid will flow –
I take it all in, just relax, breathe slow.
'We're going for the subarachnoid space,'
the anaesthetist tells me;
we're crouched, face to face,
I can smell pear soap on his skin,
fine needle in gloved hand, it's so thin…

Nine centimetres long, tightrope of stainless steel,
high-wire walk, summertime 2004,
daydreaming of the earth,
the way feet feel on floor
when we land.
Bring myself back to the room.
I'm a nurse, blue scrub costume,
not here to write poems, I know that, I know –
just relax, just relax, breathe slow.

The man on the trolley is calm.
I watch fluid being warmed,
then travel through tubes up his arm;

that fuzzy feeling in your veins
when you've had a few,

we're young again, and everything is new,
drunk on James' homemade brew,
it tastes like rubber, burnt balloons,
and my phone is flashing,
Mum's calling, got to leave soon,
but just look at the moon,
can't leave –

I can see my face up there!
Silver, black moon stains,
distorted like the back of a spoon.
Bring myself back to the room.
I'm a nurse, blue scrub costume,
not here to write poems, I know that, I know –
just relax, breathe slow.

So here's the procedure:
we're down on our knees,
eyeball to skin
and I watch that wavering needle
go in, go in –
no blood, just metal and skin.
Push, resistance
and then give;
out of the hub comes… liquid,
just a drop, then two.
I look at the anaesthetist. 'Is this okay? Is this new?'
'Cerebrospinal fluid,' he says; 'we've found the right spot,'
and he sticks a plaster over a pinprick-reddened dot.
The fluid starts to run:
ice shards, beads of rain glinting in the sun,
it's clearer than crystal,
like river water running over cut glass,
I've never seen something so pure and clear come to pass.
It's poetry, words running free at last;
This man's a poet! I want to shout.
But everybody's left now, there's no one about.
He's ready for theatre, the procedure is done

and I'm feeling akin with the man lying asleep and at one
with the world 'cause he's got poetry in his spine,
and I know that I can be both these things,
poet and nurse,
because if there's words there inside you,
then what's wrong with a bit of verse?

CLICK
For the Wizard of Skill

I've just heard the news
that you've passed away
and now I'm driving home
along the A20
which is just
concrete and grey.

And though it's summer in London
and the trees are emerald-leafed,
there's a willow by the side
of the overpass
that seems draped-heavy
with grief.
Or perhaps,
beyond the bridge,
past the railings
where I can't see,
maybe the catkins are golden
and the leaf-tips skim
the water,
floating and free.

I drive past Flamingo Park
with Fun Land set up for
the summer.
The carousel spins,
I watch swinging legs
that sprint to win
stuffed toys on the ring toss,
a fiver on the coconut shy,
but as the sun starts to set
I see rust and cogs and wheels
slowly turning
beneath a darkening sky.

I only met you four or five times
but enough to remember your

smile, rain-wet parka, your rhymes
that took the stage on almost
every poetry
night in London,
laid down rhythmic stanzas
that rang of the old skool,
when mix tapes and marker pens
were all you needed to be cool.
I smile, driving home, thinking of it all.

That last time,
at the Green Note café,
we were both there early,
coins out ready to pay,
ready to say words on a stage
with just a mic,
feeling like
freewheeling,
hands off handlebars,
bike wheels
ticking with beads and cards
tucked between the spoke-
n
word –
blurred-fast
unravelling words
like all the memories
that whip past
as you drift away...

Where do we go?
Where do we go
when the poetry stops?
Auden once said that
we should stop all the clocks,
that love doesn't last
forever, but I will
always remember

the Wizard of Skill,
the words he brought
and the room he would fill
with laughs and kicks;
he was the first to click
passages that moved him,
a vibration,
shuddering up to the brim,
like the first sound made
when the world
began to spin:
click,
I click you goodnight
and click you for the
poems you were still yet to write.
Click for the family you've left behind
and click for all the smiles
you've left like
cassette ribbon
in people's minds.

OPERATING THEATRE LOVE POEM

Working in operating theatres is boring;
listening to the sedated sounds
of other people snoring,
scoring every measurable
detail in numbers,
balancing carbon dioxide
in slumbers.
Counting swabs to make sure
none are left inside,
one, two, three,
those bloody ones left on the side.
Time passes slowly
so I think of something to do
and it revolves around an 'I spy' method
that includes me and you.

I guess some might say it's gruesome
to look for reminders of you in here,
the skin flap,
the bone shave,
the ear with a swirl
that looks just like your smile
on a warm summer's evening…
in Hyde Park…
by the bandstand…
if I look really hard.

So you're in here,
in the cool of the operating room,
entombed with the cholecystectomy bloke
knocked out
beneath the blue sheet,
which we once had:
Primark ones that wouldn't cover your feet –
faux satin sheets as blue as a duck egg,
and when we made love
one of us would slide onto the floor,
sitting bolt upright,
facing the door.

I suppose it's obvious to say
the *pyramids* remind me of you?
We have these crystal-filled pyramids
with a tube running through.
Turns fluids to solids:
urine and pus,
bile and blood –
the floods of the Nile tour with Gary!
(Who was not Egyptian.)
What a wonderful holiday that was;
sun, sand, mysterious encryptions.

I got to watch rapid sequence today –
that reminded me of you.
It's basically a technique
to stop stomach contents
leaking through.
Up and out the oesophagus,
projectile vomiting on the ceiling;
feeling for the muscle,
they push hard on the throat.

Don't you remember that time?
I was pissed and you got soaked
in my vomit?
Well, your shoes did;
I never had good aim,
and bundling me on to the train
you said, 'Please never do this again.'

There was also this first incision:
surgeon went knife to skin,
just a tiny slit to begin.
Removal of a testicle,
popped from its wattly sack;
it had grown beyond its means
and didn't know how to go back.
This procedure reminded me

of what our birth might be like:
bulbous pink Ridley Scott creation
with your nose
(our baby of the future, not the testicle)
crowning through a dark cavity
the size of this membraney plum,
defying all theories of gravity,
pushed, pushed, pushed
by the surgeon
(who wore his hat disturbingly like a chef),
me screaming till we're all deaf
and then he is born,
a swollen and oversized sphere
that we call Jeff
(the future baby, not the testicle).
In bone surgery they use power tools:
blades, saws, drills and files
to smooth a fractured femur
and something called a reamer
colloquially known as the cheese grater.
Seeing bone being grated into neat white filings
did remind me of our fine dining in Rome:
flecks of parmesan, spaghetti, macchiato foam,
strolling the streets away from the stresses of home.

And the new ceramic hip is held up to the light,
sparkling as if scattered with quartz it's so bright;
unfortunately it looks like a golf ball – perfectly the same.
It's a game we've never played.
There are no memories here.

This must be true love since I see you everywhere:
a urinary catheter with kinks,
like you, in the bedroom.
You're in the sound of the ventilation system
that seems to whisper my name
and when it comes to going home,
I feel like you've been with me all day.

THE THINGS YOU OWN

Shoes,
laceless;
the eyelets
are a dozen black whorls
in bark
staring back at you
from a park, after dark –
everybody's left now.
The tongues are hanging
like a skin flap,
trapped
in chain-link fences
too high to climb
and you shouldn't be here now;
let's go
a different way
– the motorway –
it could take you far from here.
There is the razor blade
I have to lock away;
'Today's not a shaving day,'
you say,
'there's a wink in the silver,
nah, today's not a shaving day.'
Rizla papers
as ghostly thin as frost
on the leaves outside,
rolled,
crackled between your fingers,
calloused, brackish blisters
that linger.
'I could've been a folk singer,'
you say –
your thumbs pinch potting clay –
singing Bob Dylan,
'Rainy Day Women',
'Never Let Me Go' –
you learnt this pottery technique

just a week ago.
Conker collection,
chocolate,
round as an equine eye –
'I've never cried in my life,'
you sigh –
'tear gland damage
when I was five –
Mum says I looked
through my telescope too long,
spent nights watching Mars
flickering bloodstone-strong,
framed beneath my curtainless sky;
nope, I've never known what it's like to cry.
Died once,
when they brought me in here,
said there was clear fluid
and blood leaking out my ears.
Unresponsive –
the nurses called my name,
called a relative
but nobody came.
I've been alone now
longer than I can remember;
the last time I saw anyone that mattered
was around the first of November
and the conversation soon blackened,
a dying ember
fluttering into grime.
It turned to death
and the amount of times
we'd done suicide; she cried
talking about it…
I didn't.
One final thing I want you to know:
in my dreams I only see one place
and it's Sainsbury's in the snow.
Somewhere I used to go

when I was a kid,
and everything was normal
and I'd pick up biscuits,
crisps and Coke like a pig.
Every day I want to walk
down the aisles like it's yesterday,
know that I'll be smiling,
compiling a list of groceries
normal people buy,
and I'll have more than this:
laceless shoes, blunt razor blades,
telescope memories
and other ones that fade,
no more pig pick-ups in the rain,
injections
and drugs for my brain
to keep me sane,
that get rid of those blind spots
you can't see,
the shadows and the colours
leaking differently.
I'll be more than this,
more than not enough change
for another phone call,
more than alone,
more than all of the things I've ever owned.'

UNDERNEATH THE ROSES WHERE I REMEMBERED EVERYTHING

For Gloria

Darling, that time in the garden:
tripped, fell, fractured a wrist,
lay sprawled and adrift
with the last of the light
that lolled and spilled across me,
Radio 4 drifting out on the summer breeze,
your deaf ears in the kitchen
that left me out there till evening came.
I laughed for hours,
lying there
underneath the roses
where I remembered everything
(sixty years of us!).
It was funny.
Everything was funny with you there.

With special thanks to all the people I met along the way.
Without them I couldn't have written this collection.